SEXY D

THE WAH NAILS BOOK OF NAIL ART

SHARMADEAN REID

Published in 2012 by Hardie Grant Books

Hardie Grant Books (UK)
Dudley House, North Suite
34-35 Southampton Street
London WC2E 7HF
www.hardiegrant.co.uk

Hardie Grant Books (Australia)
Ground Floor, Building 1
658 Church Street
Melbourne, VIC 3121
www.hardiegrant.com.au

British Library Cataloguing-in-Publication Data. A catalogue record
for this book is available from the British Library.

ISBN 978-174270320-6

Text copyright © Sharmadean Reid 2012
Polaroids on endpapers © Cochi Esse, Jolene Henry and Grace Ladoja
Photographs on pages 6, 7, 17, 37, 39, 45, 49, 63, 69, 73 and 88 © Grace
Ladoja
Photograph on page 4 © Jordan Stokes
Photographs on page 8 © Chloe Fiducia
Photographs on pages 19, 22, 23, 35, 27, 31, 32, 33 35, 55, 57, 61, 67, 71,
74, 75, 77, 79, 82, 83, 85 and 87 © Alex Sainsbury
Photographs on pages 28 and 29 © Tyrone Lebon
Photographs on pages 46, 47 and 96 © Jolene Henry
Photographs on pages 50 and 51 © Matt Irwin
Collage pages 58 and 59 © Loren Platt
Photograph on page 95 © Carl Pidlaoan
Polaroid and real film photographs on pages 17, 19, 29, 43, 45, 49, 63, 69,
73 © Cochi Esse
WAH 100 nails illustrations © Cath Grossider
All other illustrations throughout © Jiro Bevis

Commissioning editor: Kate Pollard
Art Direction: Rob Meyers for RBPMstudio
Design: RBPMstudio
Retoucher: Steve Crozier
Proofreader: Rose Gardner

Every attempt has been made to contact copyright holders. The publishers
would like to hear from any copyright holders who may not have been
attributed.

Colour reproduction by MDP
Printed and bound in China by 1010

10 9 8 7 6 5

NOTE: None of the products that have been mentioned in this book have been
endorsed, they are simply the preferred products of the WAH Nails team.

THE *Wah* NAILS BOOK OF NAIL ART

SHARMADEAN REID

hardie grant books

About Wah

In my travels as a stylist, I'd regularly go to Marie NAILS in LA and Valley NYC in New York, and I was perplexed as to why London didn't have a cool nail salon of its own, when it's supposed to be a trendsetting city! Then, in 2008, after another bad experience at a hood salon (I wanted a Dior-esque double French, the technician didn't know what Dior was) I got home and told my boyfriend: "You know what? I'm gonna open my own nail salon!"

As I spoke the words, the ideas started flowing ... it wasn't just going to be any salon, it was going to be a community for all the local girls in my neighbourhood, and beyond. I wanted to reflect the spirit behind WAH, the online girls' fanzine I was making at the time. I had started the blog for the fanzine in 2006 and had gathered an international gang of girls who would crash at each other's houses when they were in town. It was only natural that the salon be called WAH Nails - a physical home for the online community I'd created.

It took a lot of planning and hard work, but after finding a location two minutes from my house in east London, we opened the doors to WAH Nails Dalston in July 2009. I lived in a big loft space at the time, and my friends were always inviting themselves over - fashion designers, DJs, writers, artists - so I knew I had the perfect creative clientele. Soon, the salon became a local hub for different happenings; we hosted Uffie's album party, had exhibitions by local female artists, and had a huge fundraiser for the victims of the Japanese tsunami, with all of our friends donating goods. Sometimes we would all just sit around after hours watching *Paris Is Burning* or Beyonce's tour DVD.

Within a few months we had been featured in *Vogue*, *Elle*, the *New York Times*, *i-D Magazine* ... pretty much every publication worth noting. I had no idea what I was doing, but the fashion press seemed to love it! By November, Selfridges had asked us to host a pop-up salon and in February 2010, we opened our Topshop space, in the flagship store on Oxford Street. It was a crazy whirlwind but I had achieved what I set out to do.

WAH Nails helped change the culture of nail design. Before we opened, "nail art" was a dirty word within beauty circles, something a bit tacky and ghetto - but I knew it could be more. Nail artists like Marian Newman, Sophy Robson and Jenny Longworth had been pioneering fashion-forward nail art in magazines for a while, but no one was bringing it to the mainstream. And that's where we came in. Our nail style has now been imitated globally, and our concept - from doing nails in clubs and festivals, to the way we relate to our customers - has infiltrated the nail world ... but there is so much more we still want to do!

The next step is this book, and it's what WAH is all about: sharing our passion, our style, and our technique with you - because everyone deserves hot nails.

Sharmadean Reid
Founder

SMASH-UP POLISH

NAIL FILE

TOP COAT

CLEAN-UP BRUSH

BASE COAT

CUTICLE OIL

BASE COAT

STUDS & RHINESTONES

COCKTAIL STICK

MINX

SHINE BUFFER

models own

NAIL POLISHES

NAIL ART PEN

models own
NAIL ART PEN

GLITTER POLISH

WHITE BLOCK BUFFER

Tool kit

NAIL STRIPERS

7

Prep & Finish

PREP

Step 1. To prep your nails it's important to thoroughly remove any old polish. Soak a cotton wool pad in some nail polish remover and remove any traces of polish, to create a clean base.

Step 2. File your nails to your desired shape. Get rid of any sharp or uneven edges. File using smooth, long motions towards the centre of the nail, from the sides in. Don't file furiously backwards and forwards like you're using a saw because you'll damage your nails. To make sure your nails are all the same length, line them up once you've finished filing.

Step 3. Using a buffer, buff your nails lightly to create a smooth nail bed. Buffing will also get rid of any ridges. Only buff once a week.

Step 4. It's important to dehydrate the nail before you apply the base coat – this will really make the polish stick. Use a cotton wool pad soaked in nail polish remover to get rid of any excess oil moisture or dust from buffing.

Step 5. Now you're ready to use your base coat! Apply a thin layer of base coat to each nail and leave to dry for one to two minutes. All that's left to do now is to choose your nail design!

FINISH

Once you've finished your nail art or design, wait for five minutes to apply your top coat so you don't smudge your work! Use Seche Vite top coat (WAH's fave) and apply a generous layer to the nails. Make sure your brush isn't overloaded with polish – you can remove any excess by wiping it across the neck of the polish bottle.

To perfect your work, always have a small tidy-up brush (tip: a small make-up brush, for eyes or lips, is great) to get rid of any imperfections. Dip your brush in acetone or nail polish remover and lightly dab any bits of polish on the fingers or around the nail bed.

To get rid of dry cuticles, apply a swipe of CND solar oil around them. This hydrates the area around the cuticle and leaves a nice, neat, shiny finish!

WAH fanzine #1

NAILS
GALLER
CLOTHIN
BOOKS+ZI

oon!

The day we we got the keys

Projects

16. LEOPARD

CANDYSTRIPE **18.**

HALF-MOON **22.**

24. AZTEC TRIBAL

26. HALF STRIPE

CAMOUFLAGE **30.**

BASKETCASE

34. LETTERHEAD **36.**

90S HIP HOP **38.**

POW! **42.**

FASH LIFE **44.**

48. STAINED GLASS

14

SHATTER 54.

ZEBRA 56.

60. BOWS

ROSES 62.

DRIPPY 66.

68. EYEBALL

DE STIJL 70.

GRAPHIC STRIPE 72.

LIPS 76.

78. GLITTER FADE

84. MARBLE

RHINESTONE RAIN 86.

DOUBLE STUDS 88.

TOP TIP: CUSTOMIZE THE DESIGN BY USING TWO
OR THREE DIFFERENT COLOURED DOTS, OR EVEN DOING
A THREE-STRIPED BASE WITH LEOPARD PRINT ON TOP!

Leopard

The original WAH girl leopard print is the design that made our name famous in the nail world. Sure, we didn't invent applying leopard print to nails, but we definitely took it to the next level. Leopard print is a classic — it can be grown-up chic or wild and crazy and can be painted in so many colourways that you are guaranteed to find a combination to suit you.

YOU WILL NEED >
• mint green nail polish
• white nail polish
• black nail-art pen

HOW TO >
Step 1. Paint your nails with the mint green base colour. Allow to dry.

Step 2. Take your white nail polish and, using a semi-dry brush, paint white strokes dotted around the nail, starting at the centre.

Step 3. With your black nail-art pen, make broken circles and semi-circles around the dots.

Step 4. Continue until all the white spots are outlined.

Step 5. Fill in the gaps with empty broken circles and black pen strokes.

WAHgirl no.1
Claudia

I'm 21 and a
designer (I work
mostly with PVC) and
I'm currently starting
a magazine. My best
nail experience was
when my friend Ashley
took me to get Minx
nails at WAH, in an
attempt to cheer me
up — I'd just been
massively dumped.
In an ideal world
I'd be a cat or a
millionaire.

Candystripe

They taste just like candy! Well, erm, maybe not – but they look just as sweet!

YOU WILL NEED >
• pink nail polish
• white nail striper

HOW TO >
Step 1. Paint your nails with the pink base colour. Allow to dry.

Step 2. Using the white striper, paint a thin, neat line down the centre of the nail.

Step 3. Paint a second line, keeping it to the left of the centre line, all the way to the tip. Make sure the lines are evenly spaced.

Step 4. Paint the third line to the right of the centre line.

Step 5. Continue to work your way outward, alternating between left and right, until you reach the edge of the nail. This will ensure you get an evenly striped pattern.

Rae

WAHgirl no.2

I'm 18 years old and I am at school, studying Politics, Art and English Lit. My best WAH experience was when me and my friend Dora had our Sweet Sixteen birthday party in the WAH Nails Dalston salon. Shar went mental cos somebody pulled the toilet door off its hinges. It was pretty messy!

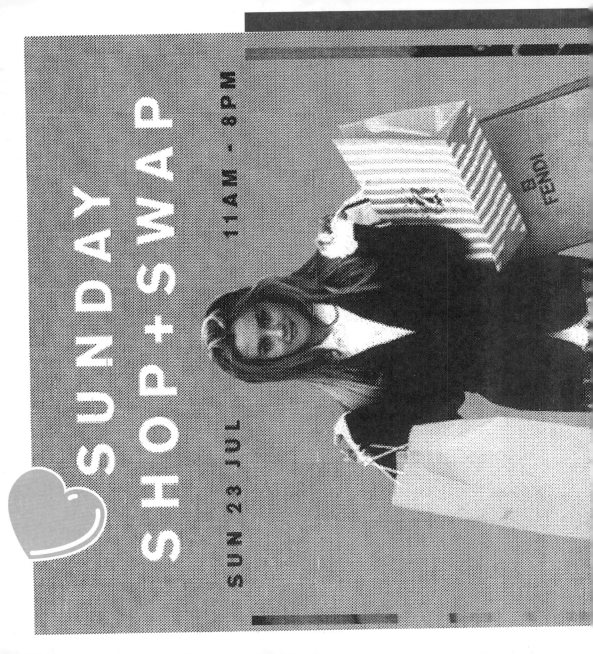

VINTAGE AND NEW CLOTHES
SHOES AND ACCESSORIES

WAH NAILS
420 KINGSLAND RD, E8

SHOP@WAH-NAILS.C

"I'm just a girl"

TOP TIP: LEOPARD PRINT HALF-MOONS LOOK AMAZING TOO! JUST FILL THE HALF-MOON AREA WITH A MINIATURE LEOPARD PRINT.

Half-Moon

Dip your finger into the world of
nail art with a classic and chic
design. Half-moons go with any
outfit; simply pick two contrasting
colours and get started.

YOU WILL NEED >
• nude nail polish
• black nail striper

HOW TO >
Step 1. Paint your nails with the nude
base colour. Allow to dry.

Step 2. Using the black striper, paint
a neat arc to emulate a "moon" near the
base of the nail.

Step 3. Still using the black striper,
paint another arc underneath that
follows the cuticle line.

Step 4. Gently sweep the striper back
and forth to fill the half moon shape
with polish.

Step 5. Gasp in wonder at your classy
nails!

Alicia

I'm 23 years old and I model my look on the hotness that is Brigitte Bardot. I'm a graphic designer obsessed with infographics; I just can't get enough of neat, clean lines! When I'm not sat at my computer I love doing jigsaw puzzles with my cat, while listening to Tom Vek or the Black Keys.

Aztec Tribal

Another original WAH design that we created back when the salon first opened in 2009! Inspired by a pair of American Apparel leggings that EVERYONE was wearing that summer, this design can be tricky but the results are outstanding!

YOU WILL NEED >
• acid green nail polish
• white nail striper
• pink nail striper
• black nail striper
• black nail-art pen
• white nail-art pen
• LOTS OF PATIENCE!

HOW TO >
Step 1. Paint your nails with the acid green base colour. Allow to dry.

Step 2. Using the white and pink stripers, paint lines across the nail in varying widths, as shown in the illustration.

Step 3. Cement the stripes using the black striper.

Step 4. Take the black nail-art pen and begin adding zig-zag lines and dashes to your design.

Step 5. Add black and white dots where appropriate, or wherever you have room!

WAHgirl no.4
Radha

I'm 26 and I'm a label manager/A&R at record label Deadly People. I DJ a lot too and run my own club night, Bounty, at the Alibi in Dalston, with my pals Kevin Morosky and Martelo. I'm obsessed with Aztec nails and have them all the time. Weird fact: me and Shar are both from the West Midlands and are both half Indian.

WAH MIX 2
WAH GIRLS RULE

Half Stripe

Bold, graphic nails for fashion-forward types. The key to this design is painting every nail differently to achieve maximum effect. Although it looks difficult, the only real skill is having a steady hand with your striper brush. So get practising those perfect lines!

YOU WILL NEED >
- coral nail polish
- white nail polish
- black nail striper

HOW TO >
Step 1. Paint half the nail with the coral base colour, differing the angle on each finger. Allow to dry.

Step 2. Paint the remainder of the nail with the white base colour. Don't worry about getting a perfect line where the colours meet at this stage. Allow to dry.

Step 3. Using your striper brush, paint a neat, even black line that divides the white from the coral.

Step 4. Working on the white half of the nail, and away from the centre line, paint a second line from the base to the tip.

Step 5. Continue to paint evenly spaced lines towards the edge of the nail until the white section is completely covered in stripes.

TOP TIP: IT'S INEVITABLE THAT YOU'LL END UP BRUSHING YOUR FINGERS WITH BLACK POLISH TO GET THE STRIPER ALL THE WAY TO THE EDGE OF THE NAIL. DON'T WORRY ABOUT THIS TOO MUCH – YOU CAN CLEAN THEM UP AFTERWARDS WITH YOUR CLEAN-UP BRUSH.

WAHgirl no.5 Phoebe

I'm a 24-year-old artist living in east London, where I was born. I work a lot with video, photography and sculpture. Recently I have been using lots of clay which ruins my nails! But I still love having them done and keeping them looking hot. I am listening to the Blood Orange record *Coastal Grooves* and the new Beyonce song "Party" pretty much on repeat at the moment. I love hanging out anywhere in London with a dancefloor and good music.

Camouflage

The camo design was inspired by one of our favourite Japanese streetwear brands, A Bathing Ape, which is famous for its camouflage prints. This looks great with three shades of the same colour or three completely contrasting colours, as we've done here.

YOU WILL NEED >
• neon yellow nail polish
• pink nail-art pen or nail polish
• blue nail-art pen or nail polish

HOW TO >
Step 1. Paint your nails with the neon yellow base colour. Allow to dry.

Step 2. Using your pink nail-art pen or pink nail polish brush, add some rounded shapes, like the ones in the illustration, at the edges of the nail. Make sure some come right off the sides of the nail so it looks like an authentic print.

Step 3. Fill in the centre with more organic shapes, being careful not to crowd the nail.

Step 4. Using your blue nail-art pen or blue polish, paint more circular shapes and blobs that slightly overlap the edges of the pink shapes.

Step 5. Check there are no huge gaps, while ensuring you leave enough room to keep the base colour visible.

I'm 24 and I do a lot of things cos I get quite bored. At the moment I make music, sometimes model and I paint nails! I get obsessed with one song for a week and then it changes the next week, but right now I'm listening to "Cult Logic" by Miike Snow & "Young Blood" by The Naked And Famous. I paint nails for some of WAH's events and parties, and by far the coolest was the Crooked Tongues BBQ Summer '11. It was nail and sneaker heaven!

"Light up the world!"

Basketcase

Zoom in on a basket weave for an abstract graphic print.

YOU WILL NEED >
• blue nail polish
• black nail striper

HOW TO >
Step 1. Paint your nails with the blue base colour. Allow to dry.

Step 2. Using the black striper brush, start at the base of the nail and paint a slightly diagonal line from the left to the right side. Maintain the same pressure on the brush from start to finish to ensure the line looks even. Lift the brush completely off the nail at the end of the line for a clean finish.

Step 3. Repeat above the first line to produce three evenly spaced stripes in black.

Step 4. Working from the tip of the nail, create three more lines, this time at a right angle to the first set.

Step 5. Finish by painting three more lines to create a triangular, woven effect!

I'm a 25-year-old writer, so obviously I wanna be the next Stephen King. When I was little I used to keep Kylie Minogue cassette tapes in a sinister red briefcase and pull them out to play when friends came over. No one but me was allowed to touch them though! My fave time at WAH was when I got Lady Carcass (AKA Lady Gaga's meat outfit) nails for Halloween. When I grow up, I wanna be Samantha Teasdale, owner of Bleach hair salon.

TOP TIP: FIND AN ACTUAL FONT TO COPY FROM SO YOU KNOW EXACTLY HOW EACH LETTER SHOULD LOOK. PRACTISE THOSE "S"S AND "R"S AS THOSE ARE THE HARDEST!

Letterhead

There's no better way to make a statement than to spell it out on your nails. The first time we did letters for a client – a super-cool graphic designer – she was so specific, she had even printed out the exact font she wanted her boyfriend's name spelled out in! Here we show you a tattoo style... So if you don't want to commit to tattooing LOVE/HATE on your knuckles, write it on your nails instead!

YOU WILL NEED >
• nude nail polish
• black nail-art pen
• white nail-art pen

HOW TO >
Step 1. Paint your nails with the nude base colour (it looks really effective if you choose one to match your skintone). Allow to dry.

Step 2. Using the black nail-art pen, start to draw the first letter, about 5 mm from the tip of the nail.

Step 3. Work your way down to about 5 mm from the base of the nail, so the letter is centred.

Step 4. When you've finished your letter, add dashes across it for a real Sailor Jerry tat vibe.

Step 5. Highlight certain parts of the letter with white pen, as shown on Gina.

WAHgirl no.8 Gina

I'm 25 years young and I work as a freelance make-up artist, but in another life I would be Tank Girl. The best WAH experience I've had was getting to do make-up for the Vans x WAH Tour. There were fly girls to hang with and I got to do make-up while touring Europe. It was pretty amazing! If I ever decide to grow up, I'd like to still be representing with some serious talons!

90s Hip Hop

An ode to the Native Tongues era of hip hop, we mix D.A.I.S.Y. Age colours with a distinct ethnic beat.

YOU WILL NEED >
• light purple nail polish
• yellow nail polish
• pink nail polish
• orange nail polish
• black nail-art pen

HOW TO >
Step 1. Paint your nails with the purple base colour. Allow to dry. Then, using the yellow nail polish, hold your brush at an angle and create short, fat brushstrokes down the centre of the nail in a diamond pattern, as shown in the illustration.

Step 2. Repeat the diamonds using the pink nail polish down the left side of the nail.

Step 3. Do the same with the orange nail polish down the right side of the nail.

Step 4. Gently squeeze the black nail-art pen and apply a thin line to outline all the diamond shapes.

Step 5. Use the pen to add dots inside each diamond and in the empty spaces.

I'm 26 and I'm a concubine. I also make an amazing TV show for *Vice* called *Fashion Week Internationale* where I check out fashion weeks from all over the world. Last week I was in Cambodia and I'm going to Nigeria next month. If I could choose to be doing anything else I would be a Rastafarian man, living in a hut in Jamaica. The best thing about WAH is knowing that no one WAHs my nails like WAH WAHs 'em!

POW!

Because we're all superwomen, we like to wow people with these POW! nails. Inspired by a love of comics and the artist Roy Lichtenstein, we came up with these nails when we first opened the salon – and it's still one of our most popular designs!

YOU WILL NEED >
• five different nail polishes
• white nail-art pen
• black nail-art pen

HOW TO >
Step 1. Paint each of your nails with a different base colour. Allow to dry.

Step 2. Paint a white "explosion" in the base corner of each nail using the white nail-art pen.

Step 3. Paint neat polka dots over the top half of the nail.

Step 4. Once each "explosion" is dry, use your black nail-art pen to write POW! CRASH! BANG! WHAM! and any other comic-book words you want within them.

Step 5. Outline the explosions with your black nail-art pen.

Simona

I am 23 years old and a nail technician at WAH. I was actually the first nail tech they hired! The best set of nails I ever did were really unique and extraordinary. The nails were pyramid shaped (also called Edge nails) in five different neon acrylic colours. They were crazy and everyone loved them! I like to go raving at Corsica Studios in London and at the moment I'm listening to anything Young Money puts out. I'm looking forward to getting my driving licence so I can go on a road trip to the USA with my friends.

Fash Life

For those on the merry-go-round that is the international fashion-week cycle, this design — a distinctive homage to the legendary artist Stephen Sprouse — should make the madness just a little bit prettier.

YOU WILL NEED >
• yellow nail polish
• pink nail polish
• orange nail polish
• black nail-art pen

HOW TO >
Step 1. Paint alternate nails with the yellow, pink and orange base colours. Allow to dry.

Step 2. Using the black nail-art pen, start at the tip by writing NEW YORK across your nail. Make sure you allow some letters to run off the edge of the nail to give it a real "print" effect.

Step 3. When you get to the edge of the nail, carry the word over to the next line. You will end up breaking words in half — but that's the idea!

Step 4. Continue down the nail, writing from left to right, adding the world's other famous fashion cities — PARIS, LONDON (obvs), TOKYO, MILAN — or whatever cities you want to rep!

I'm 23 years old and I'm studying Womenswear at the University of Westminster. My fave song at the mo' is "Under The Ivy" by Kate Bush and I like to listen to it while eating sausages. The first time I ever came into the WAH salon I met a little black dog, he was cuuutttteee! My best ever nails were Pink Camo Minx.

WAH x Vans Tour '11

Stained Glass

Go colour crazy by imitating the ancient art of stained glass with these pretty patterned nails.

YOU WILL NEED >
• yellow nail polish
• blue nail polish
• pink nail polish
• lime green nail polish
• black nail-art pen

HOW TO >
Step 1. Using your yellow nail polish brush, paint three dabs on the nail, spaced far apart. Hold the brush flat so you get a squarish mark.

Step 2. Paint a few blue dabs, close to, but not overlapping, the yellow.

Step 3. Add some pink, being careful not to touch the other colours.

Step 4. Fill in the remaining gaps with the lime green nail polish.

Step 5. Using your black nail-art pen, outline all the colours to create a stained-glass effect.

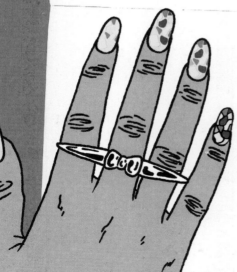

I'm 22 and I'm a body painter and performer. I love make-up but don't pluck my eyebrows. The best superhero on earth is Brienne, the Maid of Tarth, but Arnold Schwarzenegger's pretty high up on the list. My earliest memory is watching *Terminator* with my brother when I was about 4 years old. When I grow up, I wanna be able to bench more than Arnie!

Bleach London are our salon best mates and partners in crime. What we do for nails, they do for hair; if we're Lil' Kim, they're Courtney Love — two sides of the same, 90s, girl-power coin. We love them because they do the coolest hair around and influence trends internationally. They also throw fun parties in the salon and wear miniskirts with woolly jumpers.

Name and age: Sam Teasdale, 28 and Alex Brownsell, 23.

What do you do? Managing Director (Sam) and Creative Director (Alex) of Bleach.

Tell us about the story of Bleach: Well, Alex used to do my hair and we became friends, then started working together. We wanted to open a salon based around the demand for Alex's bleaching and colouring, so we drew up some business plans. But in the end we just ended up in the back of WAH.

Who's your hero?
We have two: Gazza and Mel B.

Who's your style icon?
Bananarama.

Biggest influences?
Lady Di and Donald Trump.

Describe your aesthetic:
Skank chic.

Fave hair you've ever done?
Hilary Alexander's purple highlights.

Fave hair look of all time?
Flock of seagulls/Lady Di/Donald Trump.

Fave WAH Nails experience:
Our Halloween hair and nails shoot.

What's your fave look at the moment?
Spray tan.

Hottest new clothing purchase?
"Blonde Ambition" tour bomber jacket and Chloe wedge boots.

Perfect Bleach playlist?
TLC — "Unpretty"; All Saints — "War of Nerves"; Katie Price and Peter Andre — "A Whole New World"; Florence and The Machine — "Never Let Me Go; Cyndi Lauper — Good Enough".

Fave place to go out?
Anywhere on the strip on Kingsland Road in Dalston

Bleach

WAH LEOPARD PRINT   POLKA BOWS   AZTEC PRINT   ANCHORS   BRETON STRIPES   STARS AND STRIPES   TUXEDO   FLUFFY CLOUDS   MARBLE MIX

DAISIES   CHEVRONS   LETTERS   PALM TREES   RAINBOW TRIBAL   PYRAMID STUDS   DRIPPY   POW!

BASKETCASE   FUNNY BONES   ART DECO   GLITTER FADE   KILT   ROSES   HALF STRIPE   PRETTY EYE   YING YANG

FACES   OMBRE   TRIUMVIRATE   DOWNTOWN   TEETH   LOVE CHILD   HOUNDSTOOTH   FLASH

EK FOREVER   EXCLAMATIONS   ARGYLE   RUFF DIAMONDS   RUNWAY   PERFECT PAISLEY   EARTHQUAKE   DOUBLE FRENCH   FADE AWAY

STAINED GLASS NAILS   DON'T WORRY BE HAPPY   SKULL + CROSS BONES   POLKA DOTS   DOMINO   ONE LOVE   STUDDED EGYPTIAN   HALF ZEBRA

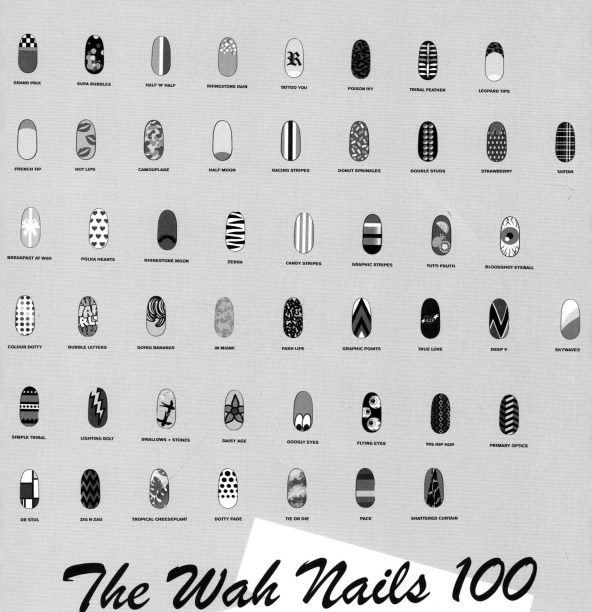

GRAND PRIX

SUPA BUBBLES

HALF 'N' HALF

RHINESTONE RAIN

TATTOO YOU

POISON IVY

TRIBAL FEATHER

LEOPARD TIPS

FRENCH TIP

HOT LIPS

CAMOUFLAGE

HALF MOON

RACING STRIPES

DONUT SPRINKLES

DOUBLE STUDS

STRAWBERRY

TARTAN

BREAKFAST AT WAH

POLKA HEARTS

RHINESTONE MOON

ZEBRA

CANDY STRIPES

GRAPHIC STRIPES

TUTTI FRUTTI

BLOODSHOT EYEBALL

COLOUR DOTTY

BUBBLE LETTERS

GOING BANANAS

IN MIAMI

FASH LIFE

GRAPHIC POINTS

TRUE LOVE

DEEP V

SKYWAVES

SIMPLE TRIBAL

LIGHTING BOLT

SWALLOWS + STONES

DAISY AGE

GOOGLY EYES

FLYING EYES

90S HIP HOP

PRIMARY OPTICS

DE STIJL

ZIG N ZAG

TROPICAL CHEESEPLANT

DOTTY FADE

TIE OR DIE

PACE

SHATTERED CURTAIN

The Wah Nails 100

TOP TIP: YOU MUST WAIT FOR YOUR BASE COAT TO DRY COMPLETELY BEFORE APPLYING THE SMASH-UP. IF YOU DON'T, IT WON'T WORK, SO GO WATCH A FEW SCENES FROM *CLUELESS* TO KILL SOME TIME.

Shatter

Shatter-effect polish is one of the latest innovations in nail technology and we love experimenting with different ways to use it! Try this background fade effect for super fashion-forward nails.

YOU WILL NEED >
• blue nail polish
• yellow nail polish
• cocktail stick
• black WAH Nails x Models Own Smash-Up polish

HOW TO >
Step 1. Paint the bottom part of the nail with the blue nail polish, just over the halfway mark. Use quite a lot of polish as you want it to be pretty wet.

Step 2. Paint the top half of the nail with the yellow nail polish, overlapping the blue slightly.

Step 3. While the polish is still wet, use your cocktail stick to blend the colours together on the nail to create a fade effect. Repeat steps 1–3 on each nail individually.

Step 4. Once your nails are completely dry, paint over the colour fade using your Smash-Up polish. Don't worry, you haven't ruined your nails!

Step 5. Watch in wonder and amazement as the polish splits and you get the Smash-Up effect!

I'm 25 and I'm a hair stylist at the super salon Bleach London. I did Shar's hair the day after she gave birth! I'm addicted to eating sweets and am pretty obsessed with shoes. My most recent purchase was a pair of Miu Miu glitter brogues with a crystal-studded heel! I'm a lady so I don't go clubbin' much — I'm more of a cinema and dinner kinda girl. I have two really good holidays booked for next year and I'm very excited. I'll have to start planning the nail art for them!

TOP TIP: SWITCH THE COLOURS TO ORANGE AND BLACK IF YOU FANCY TIGER STRIPES!

Zebra

Unleash your wild side with zebra-print nails. This simple design is striking and effective.

YOU WILL NEED >
- white nail polish
- black nail striper

HOW TO >
Step 1. Paint your nails with the white base colour. Allow to dry.

Step 2. Using the black striper, start at the base of the nail and paint evenly spaced stripes in black, from the left side of the nail to the centre. To do this, press down heavily on the brush as you begin at the edge of the nail, gradually releasing the pressure as you reach the centre. This will create a triangular-shaped line.

Step 3. Work your way to the tip of the nail to produce three or four evenly spaced stripes.

Step 4. Repeat on the right side of the nail, filling the gaps created by the lines just painted.

Step 5. Gawp at your seriously cute nails!

Christina

I'm 19 and I work
in fashion styling.
My fave record right
now is Vybez Kartel
"You Mi Need". When
I first got WAH'd I
got a gold/glitter/
Zebra print and I was
buzzing for a week
LOL... My style is
half hipster, half
hood: gold chains with
paisley print, space
prints, gold Minx
nails, black and white
and gold, stripes and
maybe a bit more gold!
Weird fact: as a
child, I actually
lived next door to
the WAH BO$$ Lady,
Sharmadean, back in
Wolverhampton.

"More than a woman"

Bows

Perfectly pretty fingertips get
wrapped up in bows. Pick light and
girly colours for maximum sweetness.

YOU WILL NEED >
• mint nail polish
• pink nail polish
• white nail striper/nail-art pen
• black nail-art pen

HOW TO >
Step 1. Paint your nails alternately
with the mint and pink nail polish.
Allow to dry.

Step 2. With the white striper, paint
a cross near the tip of each nail.

Step 3. Still using the white
striper, paint vertical lines to
connect the cross, to making a bow
shape.

Step 4. Fill in the bow with white polish.

Step 5. Squeeze your white nail-art
pen until a tiny white ball of polish
forms on the end of the nib. Stop
squeezing and gently touch the ball
into the middle of the bow, pushing it
out to create a circle in the centre.

Step 6. Outline the whole bow using
your black nail-art pen. Finish it by
adding two pinch lines off the middle
of each bow.

I'm 22 years old and I'm a nail technician at WAH Nails, working in the Oxford Circus branch. Beyoncé is basically the best pop star out there right now, and I'm listening to "Countdown" on repeat. My friends, family and boyfriend make me happy but my leather jacket does a pretty good job of it too. Obviously I've done hundreds of nail designs at work, but my fave is double studs on a nude base. For the future I'm going to keep working hard, learning everything I can and hopefully be the best nail tech in the world!!!

Roses

Wake up and smell 'em! These nails are pretty as pie and are just beautiful on a spring day!

YOU WILL NEED >
- white nail polish
- pink nail polish
- lilac nail polish
- red nail polish
- green nail polish
- black nail-art pen

HOW TO >
Step 1. Paint your nails with two coats of the white base colour. Allow to dry.

Step 2. Paint a dab of pink in the middle of the nail, a dab of lilac at the tip and a dab of red at the base, alternating on each nail.

Step 3. Add some green leaves by gently using the corner of the polish brush to create a triangle effect.

Step 4. Loosely outline the coloured circles and leaves using your black nail-art pen.

Step 5. Finish by adding semi-circles in the centre of the rose to create a petal effect.

I'm 22 and I'm in my final year studying fashion design. I like making cute backpacks and amazing biker jackets. In another life I would be Lisa "Left-Eye" Lopes (RIP) or one of the sexy club girls in my fave film, *Belly.* My best WAH experience was getting my nails done with my friend Ashley, while at the same time watching *Clueless,* drinking tea and eating chocolate! My ambition is to have my own shop selling clothes :D

WAH MIX 2
WAH GIRLS RULE

1. NENEH CHERRY – "BUFFALO STANCE"
2. TECHNOTRONIC – "PUMP UP THE JAM"
3. BEYONCÉ – "UPGRADE U"
4. KELIS – "BOSSY"
5. JENNIFER LOPEZ – "JENNY FROM THE BLOCK"
6. L7 – "SHOVE"
7. HOLE – "CELEBRITY SKIN"
8. GWEN STEFANI – "HOLLABACK GIRL"
9. BRITNEY – "I'M A SLAVE 4 YOU"
10. CRISTINA – "DISCO CLONE"
11. MADONNA – "JUSTIFY MY LOVE"
12. M.I.A. – "BAMBOO BANGA"

Drippy

One of our original, and favourite, designs! Sometimes inspiration comes from the products themselves and we came up with this design when we were given the most delicious, chocolately nail polish we'd ever seen! We swiftly created an ice-cream drip nail and since then we've changed the colours to create green slime, red blood and pink paint. It's a real hit with our clientele.

YOU WILL NEED >
• pink nail polish
• black nail-art pen

HOW TO >
Step 1. Paint your nails with the pink base colour. Allow to dry.

Step 2. Using your black nail-art pen, start near the bottom of the nail and paint the outline of a long drip and a mini drip.

Step 3. Continue to paint a long, fat drip in the middle.

Step 4. End the drips with some of smaller in length, making each finger different for a unique effect.

Step 5. Squeeze the nail pen out to fill the drippy area with solid black. You can add some smaller splats off the main one for a cool variation!

TOP TIP: WHEN YOU'VE MASTERED THIS, YOU CAN TRY ADDING REAL DRIPS USING JUST THE NAIL-POLISH BRUSH WITH EXCESS POLISH ON IT!

WAHgirl no.17

Charlotte

THE MUSHPIT

ISSUE #1

I'm 22 and I do a little bit of everything. I assist Shar on shoots with styling and casting. I've also just made a fanzine with my flatmate Bertie called The Mushpit. It's about girls, fashion and boys – basically a mag for those of us who still feel like 17-year-olds but aren't! Oh, and I'm doing an English and Media degree at Goldsmiths. "212" by Azealia Banks is on my iPod right now; I love her. My best WAH experience was going on the Vans tour with all the WAH girls crew; we went to Amsterdam, Berlin and Milan. It was hella hectic and HELLA FUN!

Eyeball

This one's not just for Halloween!
Get gruesome with these bloodshot
eyeballs!

YOU WILL NEED >
• white nail polish
• blue nail-art pen
• black nail-art pen
• white nail-art pen
• red nail-art pen

HOW TO >
Step 1. Paint your nails with the
white base colour. It can get messy
so don't go too close to your cuticles
and skin. Allow to dry.

Step 2. Using the blue nail-art pen,
draw a circle outline in the centre
of the nail. Next, gently squeeze nail
polish out of the nail-art pen to fill
the circle completely.

Step 3. Add a smaller black circle in the
centre, using the black nail-art pen.

Step 4. Squeeze your white nail pen
until a tiny white ball of polish forms
on the end of the nib. Stop squeezing
and gently touch the ball onto the side
of the black dot. Make sure the nib
itself doesn't touch the nail, just
the ball of polish. This will add a
reflection spot on your eyeball.

Step 5. Take your red nail-art pen
and work inwards from the edge of the
nail to create the blood veins. Make
lightning-bolt and Y-shaped jagged lines
to make them look authentic.

I'm 31 and I'm the director and designer of CASSETTEPLAYA. Dog costumes make me happy, but any music by Kingdom does a pretty good job of it too. The hottest item of clothing I bought this year was a fake-fur leopard-print coat which was pure Patricia Arquette in the movie *True Romance*. I have been getting my nails done at WAH since it first opened and my fave designs were BAPE Camo and 3D ice-creams... My best WAH experience was seeing the WAH team doing nails at the CASH Money party!

De Stijl

Many art movements have inspired us in our designs but this infamous Dutch painting looked so good, we applied it, literally.

YOU WILL NEED >
- white nail polish
- red nail striper
- blue nail striper
- yellow nail striper
- black nail-art pen

HOW TO >
Step 1. Paint your nails with the white base colour. Allow to dry.

Step 2. Using your red striper, draw a large square outline on the left side of the nail, that takes up about a third of the nail area. Fill in the square with red.

Step 3. Take your blue striper and create a smaller blue triangular shape at the bottom of the nail that just touches the red square. Fill in with blue. Use your yellow striper to create a small yellow triangle at the tip of the nail, not quite touching the red square, and fill in with yellow.

Step 4. Once the colours are dry, use your black nail-art pen to draw straight lines between the red, yellow and blue shapes, so that they are all outlined.

Step 5. To finish, add a small black outline under the yellow triangle and two small vertical lines under the red square.

Coralie

I'm into what I call "split creativity" – I do a bit of everything! I regularly go to Mother's Meetings, a cool mum's crew, set up by graphic designer Jenny Scott, which is where I met Shar and her baby boy, Roman. Like Shar I'm a working mum so I've treated myself to some banging Louboutins this year. My fave WAH nails has gotta be the ones I got for the book shoot. They're da bomb!

Graphic Stripe

TOP TIP: IF YOU HAVE SHORT NAILS, YOU COULD EASILY SWITCH THIS DESIGN TO RUN VERTICALLY, WHICH WOULD GIVE THE APPEARANCE OF LENGTHENING YOUR NAIL BED.

Sometimes you just gotta get serious with your nails and stripes are a fail-safe way to do that. We've gone for black, gold and pink, our fave colour combo, but these would look even more sombre and graphic in a monotone.

YOU WILL NEED >
• gold nail polish
• white nail polish
• pink nail striper
• black nail striper

HOW TO >
Step 1. Paint your nails alternately with the gold and white base colours. Allow to dry.

Step 2. Using your pink striper, paint a neat straight line across the bottom third of your nail. Fill in to your cuticle area using the tip of your striper brush.

Step 3. In the top third of your nail, repeat using the black striper.

Step 4. Still using the black striper, paint a straight horizontal line in the centre of the nail.

Step 5. Pull out your pink striper again to add a fine pink line just under your black block at the tip of your nail.

Suzannah

I'm 25 and an artist. I also co-founded creative emporium Over It & Co. I had my first solo show in WAH Nails, Dalston, which was pretty amazing. The most crazed WAH experience was having my nails done in the middle of the Tate Britain for the Chris Ofili-inspired event "Bring The Noise". My nails looked like they had magical powers! I'm gonna aim to spend next year following my life mantra: Make Art with Intregrity. Have Fun. See the World.

Name: Jenny On

Age: 23

What you do: I work directly under Sharmadean, managing the WAH empire.

Tell us about how you started at WAH: I went into WAH in Dalston for the first time in 2009, with a few friends who knew Sharmadean. We got talking and she asked if I was interested in working at their month-long pop-up concession in Topshop, Oxford Circus. Of course I agreed. The pop-up became permanent and eighteen months later, so was I.

Talk us through a typical day at WAH HQ: At WAH HQ, there is never a "typical" day, I wish there was! I find that I'll go into work, have my to-do list in front of me, make a coffee, then just as I think it will be an easy day, something such as a last-minute shoot will get scheduled in, or a missing delivery will arrive. WAH is a fast-paced environment, so I don't know any different anymore! But I'm not complaining: it means I'm always on the go and it's never boring in the world of WAH.

What's the best thing about your job? There's always something new to work towards. When a new project or collaboration comes up, I literally can't help but turn into a teenage girl from all the excitement. Also, the best thing about working for WAH Nails is the fact that we are actually the BEST at what we do. What more can I say!

And the hardest thing? With my position, the most difficult is keeping up the standard of work for the company, staff and most importantly, my boss!

Describe the WAH aesthetic in a few words: Uptown meets downtown.

Who's your style icon? I don't have one person in particular. I do think I'm very lucky to have been brought up in London, where everyone is wearing something interesting, whichever part you live in.

Biggest influences? Everyone important around me.

Fave nails of all time? Monochrome "EK FOREVER" nails from our menu. They're amazing and go with everything.

What's new for nails in the future? With WAH, anything is possible!

Fave WAH nails experience: Everytime Sharmadean suddenly shouts out onto the streets "HELLO, DALSTON!"

What's on your mind right now? "What I am wearing tonight?!"

What's your fave look at the moment? Short leather skirts or long maxis with boots. All black of course.

Hottest item of clothing you've bought recently? My black denim overalls. I'll wear them with boots to work in, and wear with heels to play in...

Perfect WAH playlist? Hip hop!

Fave place to go out? I always end up back in East London. East has the best restaurants and do the best Vietnamese and Caribbean food. And the warehouse parties are always loads of fun.

What are you looking forward to for the future? More accomplishments and happy memories.

WAH's Manager Jenny

Lips

Depending on the size and length of the nail, you may be able to get two to three sets of lips on each one. Have a picture of some lips on hand to draw from, to help you create the right shape. You can also experiment with colours – black lips on a pink base look amaze!

YOU WILL NEED >
• pink nail polish
• red nail striper

HOW TO >
Step 1. Paint your nails with the pink base colour. Allow to dry.

Step 2. Get your red nail-art pen and test the colour quickly on a paper towel. You want to get rid of any air bubbles in the pen.

Step 3. Draw the outline of a set of lips towards the bottom of the nail, at a slight angle.

Step 4. Fill in the lips with the red nail-art pen, leaving a small gap in the middle for the mouth and taking care not to go outside your outline.

Step 5. Repeat this two more times on the nail. Start drawing your second set of lips in the middle of the nail, at an opposing angle to the one at the bottom, and fill them in. Draw your final lips at the tip of the nail at a differing angle again, then fill them in as above.

I'm a 17-year-old student and I'm also a "Burgerette" with the legendary London burger company, Meatwagon. As much as I hate to admit it, I've pretty much got Drake on lock right now. My loves? Food, and my amazing boyfriend. Next year I wanna go spend some time in New York again cos last year me, Mollie and Shar tore it up. Best WAH nails? Camo claws!

Glitter Fade

Sometimes you just need a bit of sparkle to make life okay. Try this quick and easy design for an instant update to plain nails.

YOU WILL NEED >
• black nail polish
• gold glitter nail polish

HOW TO >
1. Paint your nails with the black base colour. Allow to dry.

2. Load up your glitter polish brush and blob the glitter along the tip of the nail.

3. Wipe the polish brush clean on the rim of the bottle, so it's almost dry, and then starting from the centre, drag the polish down towards the cuticle.

4. Continue with the left-side of the nail, dragging the glitter polish from the tip, down towards the cuticle with the dry brush, to create the fade.

5. Drag right edge down to the cuticle and fill in any gaps with tiny amounts of glitter.

WAHgirl no.22

Grace

I'm 26 years old and I'm a director, as well as owning a production company called Ladoja & Sons. But next year, I'm looking forward to making art and breaking hearts. My fave things in life are travelling, kids and love, but I'm also hyped over my Versace for H & M bomber and my leopard-print catsuit. Every WAH experience is the best. No joke. I love experimenting with new designs and products, and the best nails I've ever had are my Jean-Michel Basquiat-style nails. In London, the best raves to go to are the underground basement raves and dancehalls! Anything that Rodigan is DJing at basically.

YOUR Sassy BLACK FRIEND

WAH fanzine #3

"Work it out"

Marble

TOP TIP: THIS DESIGN LOOKS BEST WITH BLACK, WHITE AND ANY OTHER COLOUR. DON'T DRAG MORE THAN THREE LINES IN EITHER DIRECTION OR IT WILL JUST LOOK LIKE A MESS!

Do one nail at a time on this one, as you want your polish to be wet when you start to create the marble effect.

YOU WILL NEED >
- beige nail polish
- white nail polish
- black nail polish
- cocktail stick

HOW TO >

Step 1. Paint your nails with the beige base colour. Allow to dry.

Step 2. Take your white nail polish and use the brush to add three blobs of polish to the nail.

Step 3. Add a couple of black polish blobs to the nail. You don't have to be really precise with this part, as marble nails look best when they aren't all uniform.

Step 4. Drag a cocktail stick vertically across the nail to create three marbled lines. Be careful not to press too hard, as your don't want to drag the base colour off the nail bed.

Step 5. Now use the cocktail stick to create three horizontal lines. Have fun with this design, it's not about being exact on this one.

Phoebe

I'm 24 and I'm a writer. My favourite WAH experiences have gotta be spending boiling hot summer days sitting outside the salon with Jenny, and dancing around to Beyoncé's "I am World" DVD for Shar's last birthday. What am I looking forward to for the future? Seeing more of the world and having as many new experiences as possible.

Rhinestone Rain

Make it rain jewels, not money, with these crystal-studded nail stars! Swarovski crystals work best with this design. Choose a dark stone, a light stone, and a white stone for a cool sparkle effect.

YOU WILL NEED >
• pink nail polish
• glitter nail polish
• nail glue
• cocktail stick
• large, medium and small rhinestones or Swarovski crystals
• top coat

HOW TO >
Step 1. Paint your nails with the pink base colour. Allow to dry, then add a light coat of glitter, fading halfway down the nail.

Step 2. Dab three drops of nail glue onto the nail. Dip your cocktail stick in some top coat, use it to pick up a large gem, then press it in place onto the nail. Follow with two more gems. The glue will take a few seconds to dry, so try not to touch them until they're secure.

Step 3. Using the same method, stick on your medium-sized rhinestones, interspersing them amongst the larger gems.

Step 4. Fill in any gaps with the small rhinestones. These little ones can be a bit fiddly to apply, but practice makes perfect!

Step 5. Add more small rhinestones trickling down the nail to get the full Rhinestone Rain effect!

86

I'm 22, and I'm a hairdresser from south London. Music-wise, I'm so into Lil' Wayne right now — his latest album has been a fave for a hot min. I work hard and play hard and am looking forward to going to Brazil next year to get some well-earned rest. I'm also a very proud mama to my little baby boy.

TOP TIP: IF YOU CANT FIND NAIL STUDS, RHINESTONES LOOK EQUALLY AS EFFECTIVE. USE BRUSH-ON NAIL GLUE IF YOU WANT YOUR STUDS TO LAST LONGER.

Double Studs

Gold on your nails will always look impressive, and these studs are surprisingly easy to apply! Find nail studs at your local craft store for an instant party look.

YOU WILL NEED >
• black nail polish
• gold studs
• cocktail stick
• top coat

HOW TO =
Step 1. Paint your nails with the black base colour. Allow to dry.

Step 2. Place a few dabs of the top coat near the base of the nail.

Step 3. Using the cocktail stick, gently touch the top coat blob on the nail - you want just a small amount on the end of your stick. Then quickly use the wet cocktail stick to pick up a stud and place two at the base of the nail on the top coat blob.

Step 4. Working away from the base, continue to place dabs of top coat and studs until the nail is full.

Step 5. Go and brush your shoulders off!

WAHgirl no.25

Gabi

I'm 27 and I do a ton of things! I work in the Nike ID lounge part-time and I'm also an actress. The best song right now is Drake feat' The Weeknd, "Crew Love" and the nails that are rocking my world are the double studs design cos I just love a bit of bling. I'm a bit of a sun queen and my idea of heaven is a very hot country with an amazing beach.

WHICH KIM ARE

YOU? WAH

4

WAH fanzine #4

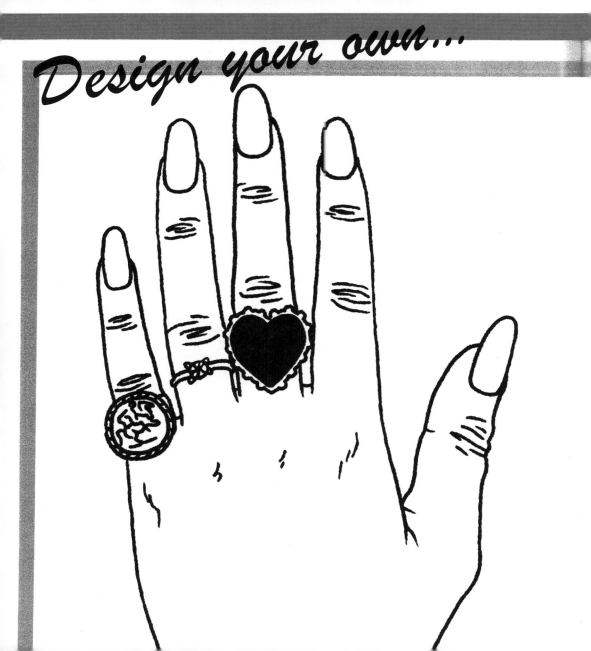

Design your own...

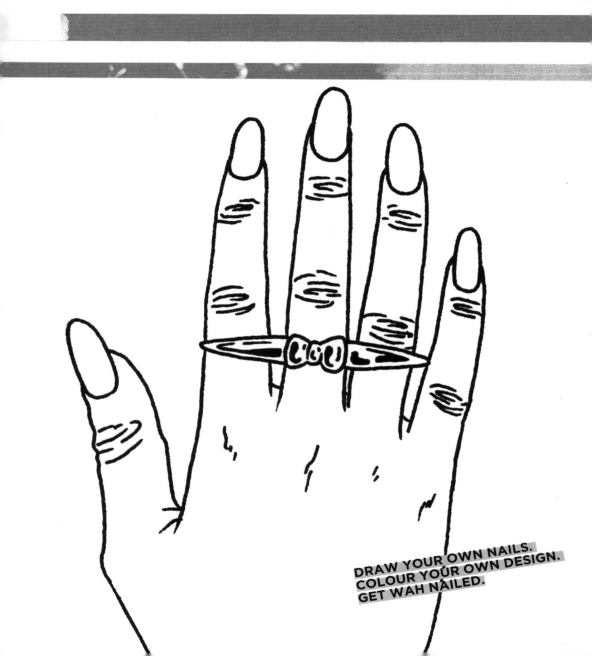

DRAW YOUR OWN NAILS.
COLOUR YOUR OWN DESIGN.
GET WAH NAILED.

Thanks

The whirlwind of WAH Nails has only been
made possible because of the following
people. Firstly, Meghan Best, one of my
best friends who started the business
with me and helped financially as well as
administratively. Without her backing,
we wouldn't exist. My other BFFs Simon,
Rosie and Grace, for wallpapering,
hanging-out and listening to my moaning.
Jenny, my right-hand woman who I'd be
lost without. My Girl Crew — Suz, Phoebe,
Hazel and Irene — for providing nails to
paint in those early days and generally
supporting everything I did. My protégé,
Charlotte, for just being an amazing
all-rounder of support. Rae and Dora,
for being cool kids and WAH Juniors.
Selfridges for giving me my big break,
and Topshop for turning that break into
a business with longevity. The Real Gold
crew for being Dalston partners in crime.
Alex, Sam and Alisha at Bleach for making
my hair dope and being the Courtney Love
to our Lil' Kim. Jennifer Byrne, Charlet
Duboc, all the girls who have featured in
this book, and my wonderful nail techs
past and present and supervisors Scarlett
and Chloe who have contributed to the
precedent that we've set with nails.
Mark, Steve and Manny at Models Own for
advice and for making our nail pen! All
of our lovely corporate clients, who
have flown us around the world, taken us
to galleries, festivals and beyond. Jiro
for his drawings, Rob for his design, and
Kate, my publisher, who gave me free rein
to do what I want — which is the only way
I like to work! And last, but by no means
least, my partner Greg who has been by my
side through painting, sanding, building,
and partying — through the good times and
the bad — I would not have been able to
have WAH Nails without him.